SUPERCHARGE YOUR DAY

Wisdom Nuggets for 365 Days of Intentional Living

NKECHI AJAEROH

Copyright © 2018 by Nkechi Ajaeroh, Just Positude Co. LLC

All rights reserved.

This book or any portion thereof may not be reproduced or used in any manner whatsoever without the prior written permission of the publisher except for the use of brief quotations in a book review, journal or article.

ISBN 978-0-9981040-3-4
Printed in the United States of America.
First Printing, 2018
Just Positude Company, LLC
P. O. Box 5394
Williamsburg, VA, 23188
www.justpositude.com www.nkechiajaeroh.com

Author's social media platforms:
www.twitter.com/honestlykechi
www.periscope.tv/honestlykechi
www.facebook.com/1honestlykechi
Email: triumph@justpositude.com

DEDICATION

This book is dedicated to everyone who seek to become better on daily basis.

INTRODUCTION

As human beings, we are faced daily with mountains of tasks to do. Sometimes it becomes so numerous that we become overwhelmed and forget the most pressing needs. At other times, we may merely lack interest and motivation to follow through to the end. And that's not all. There is also the constant battle of the opportunity cost and benefits of whatever actions we decide to take verses the ones we would not take.

I am a firm believer in learning and teaching a habit of the "daily push." Some people may call this an "affirmation" or a "daily reminder." I have come to realize that a little nudge in the tush goes a long way.

This book gives daily encouragement and motivation to get you thinking about your goals so that you can become not only a dreamer but a doer. Each daily nugget brings you closer to where you want to be.

This book is designed for you to get only a nugget each day because "less is more" and a single nugget is enough. I doubt if you need another gigantic resource like an encyclopedia to remind you about your daily task. In this book, comprising of one quote a day, you will supercharge your day to take intentional actions.

Remember, you already have everything you need within you to become whoever you desire to be. This book, like any other material, is a guide but you are the driver. You will have to open it, read it and put into practice each daily teaching.

You are smart. You are intelligent. You are worth every dream in your heart. And you can do it. You can change your life and your world.

I pray this book helps you realize your worth so that you can use your wing.

Triumph!

DAY 1

> *You only have one life to live.
> Choose how you want to live it.*

Today's Three Must Do's:

1. _____

2. _____

3. _____

Today I am grateful for:

☐ _____

☐ _____

☐ _____

DAY 2

> *Believe in yourself, your strength and your abilities because you are enough to create the life you want.*

Today's Three Must Do's:

1. _____

2. _____

3. _____

Today I am grateful for:

- [ ] _____
- [ ] _____
- [ ] _____

DAY 3

> *Success does not happen by luck, chance or accident. Intentional and consistent preparation lays the groundwork for success.*

Today's Three Must Do's:

1. _____

2. _____

3. _____

Today I am grateful for:

☐ _____

☐ _____

☐ _____

DAY 4

> *As you journey, faith is paramount. When you walk by faith, everything is possible.*

Today's Three Must Do's:

1. _____

2. _____

3. _____

Today I am grateful for:

☐ _____

☐ _____

☐ _____

DAY 5

"
People may never understand the magnitude of your God-given dream or its urgency. Proceed without their permission.
"

Today's Three Must Do's:

1. _____

2. _____

3. _____

Today I am grateful for:

☐ _____

☐ _____

☐ _____

DAY 6

> *You will end up in a different destination than originally intended if you keep looking over your shoulder without focusing on your lane.*

Today's Three Must Do's:

1. _____

2. _____

3. _____

Today I am grateful for:

☐ _____

☐ _____

☐ _____

DAY 7

> *By altering what you see, you can change your life's trajectory.*

Today's Three Must Do's:

1. _____

2. _____

3. _____

Today I am grateful for:

☐ _____

☐ _____

☐ _____

DAY 8

> *It is my life, and it deserves my work.*
> *I refuse to be discouraged in my journey.*

Today's Three Must Do's:

1. _____

2. _____

3. _____

Today I am grateful for:

☐ _____

☐ _____

☐ _____

DAY 9

> *Look for progress beyond the flamboyant, physical manifestation. Instead, see improvement in your daily struggles, which eventually lead to growth.*

Today's Three Must Do's:

1. _____

2. _____

3. _____

Today I am grateful for:

☐ _____

☐ _____

☐ _____

DAY 10

> *Your perception can make you more grateful for your situation or distasteful of your situation.*

Today's Three Must Do's:

1. _____

2. _____

3. _____

Today I am grateful for:

☐ _____

☐ _____

☐ _____

DAY 11

> *Quitting does not make your job easier.*
> *It only makes it harder the next time.*

Today's Three Must Do's:

1. _____

2. _____

3. _____

Today I am grateful for:

☐ _____

☐ _____

☐ _____

DAY 12

> *In order to win, you must be willing to get ahead of time. Start now. Start early.*

Today's Three Must Do's:

1. _____

2. _____

3. _____

Today I am grateful for:

☐ _____

☐ _____

☐ _____

DAY 13

> "
> *Time does not stop nor does it wait for anyone. Proper planning makes time management easier.*
> "

Today's Three Must Do's:

1. _____

2. _____

3. _____

Today I am grateful for:

☐ _____

☐ _____

☐ _____

DAY 14

> *The first part of becoming successful is when you realize where you are and what you need to do.*

Today's Three Must Do's:

1. _____

2. _____

3. _____

Today I am grateful for:

☐ _____

☐ _____

☐ _____

DAY 15

> *The realization that you are enough is the basis to create more significant things in your life and later in the life of others.*

Today's Three Must Do's:

1. _____

2. _____

3. _____

Today I am grateful for:

☐ _____

☐ _____

☐ _____

DAY 16

> *Hope makes everything better because it helps you see beyond your circumstances and opens your eyes to what is yet to come.*

Today's Three Must Do's:

1. _____

2. _____

3. _____

Today I am grateful for:

☐ _____

☐ _____

☐ _____

DAY 17

> *You can only reap according to how much you sow. If you plant a small seed, it can only increase so much. However, a generous seeding will likely increase your harvest immensely.*

Today's Three Must Do's:

1. _____
2. _____
3. _____

Today I am grateful for:

☐ _____
☐ _____
☐ _____

DAY 18

> *Do not give your power away by allowing other people to make decisions for your life.*

Today's Three Must Do's:

1. _____

2. _____

3. _____

Today I am grateful for:

☐ _____

☐ _____

☐ _____

DAY 19

> *When you don't forgive, you allow the past experience to control your life and dictate your future.*

Today's Three Must Do's:

1. _____

2. _____

3. _____

Today I am grateful for:

☐ _____

☐ _____

☐ _____

DAY 20

> *Read a new book each month. You can never underestimate the power of reading*

Today's Three Must Do's:

1. _____

2. _____

3. _____

Today I am grateful for:

☐ _____

☐ _____

☐ _____

DAY 21

> *A wealthy mindset is indispensable and helps you see beyond your current situation.*

Today's Three Must Do's:

1. _____

2. _____

3. _____

Today I am grateful for:

☐ _____

☐ _____

☐ _____

DAY 22

> *Big goals are not for feeble-minded people. Your lofty goal deserves your courage*

Today's Three Must Do's:

1. _____

2. _____

3. _____

Today I am grateful for:

☐ _____

☐ _____

☐ _____

DAY 23

> *To grow, you must realize the intensity of work that your goals and tasks demand, and do the work without looking back.*

Today's Three Must Do's:

1. _____

2. _____

3. _____

Today I am grateful for:

☐ _____

☐ _____

☐ _____

DAY 24

> *Do not seek other people's opinion and approval because it may not serve you. Remember, other people's thoughts are not as important as your own decisions.*

Today's Three Must Do's:

1. _____

2. _____

3. _____

Today I am grateful for:

☐ _____

☐ _____

☐ _____

DAY 25

> *Set boundaries and limit your limitations.*

Today's Three Must Do's:

1. _____

2. _____

3. _____

Today I am grateful for:

☐ _____

☐ _____

☐ _____

DAY 26

> *Do not kill your chances with too many commitments! Reduce obligations to increase focus.*

Today's Three Must Do's:

1. _____

2. _____

3. _____

Today I am grateful for:

☐ _____

☐ _____

☐ _____

DAY 27

> *Successes happen after lengthy trials, errors, and most importantly, with a determined spirit.*

Today's Three Must Do's:

1. _____
2. _____
3. _____

Today I am grateful for:

- ☐ _____
- ☐ _____
- ☐ _____

DAY 28

> *Your "enough-ness" is good enough.*

Today's Three Must Do's:

1. _____

2. _____

3. _____

Today I am grateful for:

☐ _____

☐ _____

☐ _____

DAY 29

> *Start with what you have but continue to invest in yourself to improve your craft.*

Today's Three Must Do's:

1. _____

2. _____

3. _____

Today I am grateful for:

☐ _____

☐ _____

☐ _____

DAY 30

> *Look for the things that will make you feel good and pursue them, sooner rather than later. Self-care is substantial for success.*

Today's Three Must Do's:

1. _____

2. _____

3. _____

Today I am grateful for:

☐ _____

☐ _____

☐ _____

DAY 31

> *Do not accept inconsistencies in the way you show up. They will diminish your efforts*

Today's Three Must Do's:

1. _____

2. _____

3. _____

Today I am grateful for:

☐ _____

☐ _____

☐ _____

DAY 32

> *Give yourself a chance. If one dream fails, try another one.*

Today's Three Must Do's:

1. _____

2. _____

3. _____

Today I am grateful for:

☐ _____

☐ _____

☐ _____

DAY 33

> *Now is the time to get up and possess your possessions.*

Today's Three Must Do's:

1. _____

2. _____

3. _____

Today I am grateful for:

☐ _____

☐ _____

☐ _____

DAY 34

> *Get rid of shame. Do not allow it to prevent you from walking in your truth.*

Today's Three Must Do's:

1. _____

2. _____

3. _____

Today I am grateful for:

☐ _____

☐ _____

☐ _____

DAY 35

> *Manage your expectations. Remember that human beings fall short and it is not the end of life. Whenever it happens, look up to God.*

Today's Three Must Do's:

1. _____

2. _____

3. _____

Today I am grateful for:

☐ _____

☐ _____

☐ _____

DAY 36

> *Setting appropriate and necessary limits is the only way to ensure your peace of mind is intact as you run the marathon of life.*

Today's Three Must Do's:

1. _____

2. _____

3. _____

Today I am grateful for:

☐ _____

☐ _____

☐ _____

DAY 37

> *Do not wait for a particular person, gift or blessing to complete you. You are complete just the way you are – fierce and fabulous.*

Today's Three Must Do's:

1. _____

2. _____

3. _____

Today I am grateful for:

☐ _____

☐ _____

☐ _____

DAY 38

> *It is ok to ask for help when you don't know what to do. Asking for help is not a sign of weakness but a reminder that you are strong enough to acknowledge your inability.*

Today's Three Must Do's:

1. _____

2. _____

3. _____

Today I am grateful for:

☐ _____

☐ _____

☐ _____

DAY 39

> *You can create, invent, and innovate because you are blessed with creativity but you have to start.*

Today's Three Must Do's:

1. _____

2. _____

3. _____

Today I am grateful for:

☐ _____

☐ _____

☐ _____

DAY 40

> *You have enough time in a day to make a remarkable difference towards your vision and dreams daily.*

Today's Three Must Do's:

1. _____

2. _____

3. _____

Today I am grateful for:

- [ ] _____
- [ ] _____
- [ ] _____

DAY 41

> *Show up and show out. Your dream requires your showcase.*

Today's Three Must Do's:

1. _____

2. _____

3. _____

Today I am grateful for:

☐ _____

☐ _____

☐ _____

DAY 42

> *Get rid of the things that no longer serve you like toxic relationships, jobs, credit cards, your past, etc. Instead, focus on what brings you joy now".*

Today's Three Must Do's:

1. _____

2. _____

3. _____

Today I am grateful for:

☐ _____

☐ _____

☐ _____

DAY 43

> *Every day, speak intentionally to yourself. Words are compelling. The words you speak to yourself matter.*

Today's Three Must Do's:

1. _____

2. _____

3. _____

Today I am grateful for:

☐ _____

☐ _____

☐ _____

DAY 44

> *Feel your freedom today. Do not restrict yourself. Express and fly.*

Today's Three Must Do's:

1. _____

2. _____

3. _____

Today I am grateful for:

- [ ] _____
- [ ] _____
- [ ] _____

DAY 45

> *The world is waiting for your success. You provide an opportunity for others to thrive by answering your own call.*

Today's Three Must Do's:

1. _____

2. _____

3. _____

Today I am grateful for:

☐ _____

☐ _____

☐ _____

DAY 46

> *Be thankful in every situation, no matter how difficult it may seem. Remember, someone somewhere is having it worse.*

Today's Three Must Do's:

1. _____

2. _____

3. _____

Today I am grateful for:

☐ _____

☐ _____

☐ _____

DAY 47

> *Remember, rejection is universal, so do not take it personally.*

Today's Three Must Do's:

1. _____

2. _____

3. _____

Today I am grateful for:

☐ _____

☐ _____

☐ _____

DAY 48

> *Think abundantly and majestically, and never allow your mind to limit yourself.*

Today's Three Must Do's:

1. _____

2. _____

3. _____

Today I am grateful for:

☐ _____

☐ _____

☐ _____

DAY 49

> *Experiences are learning opportunities. Embrace them and learn from them.*

Today's Three Must Do's:

1. _____

2. _____

3. _____

Today I am grateful for:

☐ _____

☐ _____

☐ _____

DAY 50

> *Forgiveness helps you to find yourself.*
> *Do not hesitate with the decision to forgive.*

Today's Three Must Do's:

1. _____

2. _____

3. _____

Today I am grateful for:

- ☐ _____
- ☐ _____
- ☐ _____

DAY 51

> *An intention without a goal cannot work. A goal without a plan cannot work. A plan without the actual action cannot work. WORK YOUR PLAN.*

Today's Three Must Do's:

1. _____

2. _____

3. _____

Today I am grateful for:

☐ _____

☐ _____

☐ _____

DAY 52

> *Only you have the power to change your situation because you are in charge.*

Today's Three Must Do's:

1. _____

2. _____

3. _____

Today I am grateful for:

☐ _____

☐ _____

☐ _____

DAY 53

> *You will only triumph when you persist without giving into the temptations of quitting.*

Today's Three Must Do's:

1. _____

2. _____

3. _____

Today I am grateful for:

☐ _____

☐ _____

☐ _____

DAY 54

> *You set the bar high by aiming high and going high.*

Today's Three Must Do's:

1. _____

2. _____

3. _____

Today I am grateful for:

☐ _____

☐ _____

☐ _____

DAY 55

> *When trying again today, give it all you've got. Your success requires your commitment.*

Today's Three Must Do's:

1. _____

2. _____

3. _____

Today I am grateful for:

☐ _____

☐ _____

☐ _____

DAY 56

> *For every mountain, you are willing to climb remember, there is a price you must be ready to pay.*

Today's Three Must Do's:

1. _____

2. _____

3. _____

Today I am grateful for:

☐ _____

☐ _____

☐ _____

DAY 57

> *Doors will open when you knock, not when you watch.*

Today's Three Must Do's:

1. _____

2. _____

3. _____

Today I am grateful for:

☐ _____

☐ _____

☐ _____

DAY 58

> *Be an encourager, but most importantly, encourage yourself.*

Today's Three Must Do's:

1. _____

2. _____

3. _____

Today I am grateful for:

☐ _____

☐ _____

☐ _____

DAY 59

> *Work on your relationships because they pay off in the long term. The right relationship produces loyalty.*

Today's Three Must Do's:

1. _____

2. _____

3. _____

Today I am grateful for:

☐ _____

☐ _____

☐ _____

DAY 60

> *Life may seem hard and dark at this time, but it only gets better if you keep pushing.*

Today's Three Must Do's:

1. _____

2. _____

3. _____

Today I am grateful for:

☐ _____

☐ _____

☐ _____

DAY 61

> *What determines what you become is going entirely in for your goals and not giving in to excuses.*

Today's Three Must Do's:

1. _____

2. _____

3. _____

Today I am grateful for:

- [ ] _____
- [ ] _____
- [ ] _____

DAY 62

> *When a door is closed, you push it open, keep knocking for someone to open it, or you turn away. The question is what are you going to do?*

Today's Three Must Do's:

1. _____

2. _____

3. _____

Today I am grateful for:

- [ ] _____
- [ ] _____
- [ ] _____

DAY 63

> *When you are faithful in pursuing your dream, the result will amaze you, and the experiences will change you.*

Today's Three Must Do's:

1. _____

2. _____

3. _____

Today I am grateful for:

- [ ] _____
- [ ] _____
- [ ] _____

DAY 64

> *Improve your knowledge, but do not be afraid to tell people that you don't know when you really don't know. Don't fake it. Learn it.*

Today's Three Must Do's:

1. _____

2. _____

3. _____

Today I am grateful for:

☐ _____

☐ _____

☐ _____

DAY 65

> *When all you have is one life,*
> *do all you can to make it work.*

Today's Three Must Do's:

1. _____

2. _____

3. _____

Today I am grateful for:

☐ _____

☐ _____

☐ _____

DAY 66

> *Be willing to adapt because situations change. Things do not stay the same.*

Today's Three Must Do's:

1. _____

2. _____

3. _____

Today I am grateful for:

☐ _____

☐ _____

☐ _____

DAY 67

> *When you show up for others, you are telling them to trust you.*

Today's Three Must Do's:

1. _____

2. _____

3. _____

Today I am grateful for:

☐ _____

☐ _____

☐ _____

DAY 68

> *You have higher chances of success when you conclude one goal before starting another. Working on too many goals at the same time can cause distractions.*

Today's Three Must Do's:

1. _____

2. _____

3. _____

Today I am grateful for:

☐ _____

☐ _____

☐ _____

DAY 69

> *Don't be arrogant because you can give more than others. Be grateful for the opportunity to serve others.*

Today's Three Must Do's:

1. _____

2. _____

3. _____

Today I am grateful for:

☐ _____

☐ _____

☐ _____

DAY 70

> *Know what you want to change in your business, relationship or any area of your life and then go for it. It is harder to change what you don't know.*

Today's Three Must Do's:

1. _____

2. _____

3. _____

Today I am grateful for:

☐ _____

☐ _____

☐ _____

DAY 71

> *Love yourself and what you bring to the table. You set the standard on how to treat you.*

Today's Three Must Do's:

1. _____

2. _____

3. _____

Today I am grateful for:

☐ _____

☐ _____

☐ _____

DAY 72

> *You must have self-control and moderation to help keep you in check.*

Today's Three Must Do's:

1. _____

2. _____

3. _____

Today I am grateful for:

- [ ] _____
- [ ] _____
- [ ] _____

DAY 73

> *Today is a good day to start. It is never wrong to go back and pursue that dream, idea, passion and vision that you always wanted.*

Today's Three Must Do's:

1. _____

2. _____

3. _____

Today I am grateful for:

- ☐ _____
- ☐ _____
- ☐ _____

DAY 74

> *After writing your goals down, keep them in front of you to get your conscious and subconscious mind aware of it.*

Today's Three Must Do's:

1. _____

2. _____

3. _____

Today I am grateful for:

☐ _____

☐ _____

☐ _____

DAY 75

> *You do not have to be an expert to provide value, but you do have to provide value or solve a problem.*

Today's Three Must Do's:

1. _____

2. _____

3. _____

Today I am grateful for:

- [ ] _____
- [ ] _____
- [ ] _____

DAY 76

> *Believe in your ability to take the necessary cause of action, and then take the ACTION to solidify your ability.*

Today's Three Must Do's:

1. _____

2. _____

3. _____

Today I am grateful for:

☐ _____

☐ _____

☐ _____

DAY 77

> *Life is a journey. Whenever you take a stumble, take a breath and continue again.*

Today's Three Must Do's:

1. _____

2. _____

3. _____

Today I am grateful for:

☐ _____

☐ _____

☐ _____

DAY 78

> *Self-awareness and self-understanding precedes goal setting.*

Today's Three Must Do's:

1. _____

2. _____

3. _____

Today I am grateful for:

☐ _____

☐ _____

☐ _____

DAY 79

> *Chase your dream and not the fame.*
> *The right dream will bring the right tribe.*

Today's Three Must Do's:

1. _____

2. _____

3. _____

Today I am grateful for:

☐ _____

☐ _____

☐ _____

DAY 80

> *Any time is a great time to start taking actions towards the goals that you wish to get accomplished.*

Today's Three Must Do's:

1. _____

2. _____

3. _____

Today I am grateful for:

☐ _____

☐ _____

☐ _____

DAY 81

> *Do not allow indecision to disrupt your future.*

Today's Three Must Do's:

1. _____

2. _____

3. _____

Today I am grateful for:

☐ _____

☐ _____

☐ _____

DAY 82

> *When perfection comes knocking, remember that done is better than perfect.*

Today's Three Must Do's:

1. _____

2. _____

3. _____

Today I am grateful for:

☐ _____

☐ _____

☐ _____

DAY 83

> *Sometimes it gets worse to get better. Trust your gut, your journey, and your judgment. Most importantly, be patient.*

Today's Three Must Do's:

1. _____

2. _____

3. _____

Today I am grateful for:

☐ _____

☐ _____

☐ _____

DAY 84

> *Be open and willing to learn from others who may know more than you on a given subject. No one knows it all.*

Today's Three Must Do's:

1. _____

2. _____

3. _____

Today I am grateful for:

☐ _____

☐ _____

☐ _____

DAY 85

> *Treat your customers right. You do not need certificates or qualifications to know right and wrong. You only need a heart of gold.*

Today's Three Must Do's:

1. _____

2. _____

3. _____

Today I am grateful for:

☐ _____

☐ _____

☐ _____

DAY 86

> *When they say, "focus on your lane," it means, "focus on your journey." You do not live other people's lives and you cannot run their race. Therefore, focus on the track you are running -- YOUR RACE.*

Today's Three Must Do's:

1. _____

2. _____

3. _____

Today I am grateful for:

- [ ] _____
- [ ] _____
- [ ] _____

DAY 90

> *Can you be everywhere and everything for everyone? The answer is no. If you try to be everywhere and everything, you will lose yourself.*

Today's Three Must Do's:

1. _____
2. _____
3. _____

Today I am grateful for:

- ☐ _____
- ☐ _____
- ☐ _____

DAY 91

"

Life will always get in the way of your goals; crying about it and beating yourself up is never the right answer.

"

Today's Three Must Do's:

1. _____

2. _____

3. _____

Today I am grateful for:

☐ _____

☐ _____

☐ _____

DAY 92

> *To win, you must start by telling yourself the truth because your win begins within.*

Today's Three Must Do's:

1. _____

2. _____

3. _____

Today I am grateful for:

☐ _____

☐ _____

☐ _____

DAY 93

> *Learn how to maintain momentum in the face of adversity. Do at least one task daily that leads to your goal.*

Today's Three Must Do's:

1. _____

2. _____

3. _____

Today I am grateful for:

☐ _____

☐ _____

☐ _____

DAY 94

> *What are your excuses costing you?*
> *Excuses cost more than action.*

Today's Three Must Do's:

1. _____

2. _____

3. _____

Today I am grateful for:

☐ _____

☐ _____

☐ _____

DAY 95

> *Summon courage and take your first step towards your goal today. Don't stop. Keep going.*

Today's Three Must Do's:

1. _____

2. _____

3. _____

Today I am grateful for:

☐ _____

☐ _____

☐ _____

DAY 96

> *Have you taken inventory of your situation lately? Remember, you must be aware of what's happening in your life.*

Today's Three Must Do's:

1. _____

2. _____

3. _____

Today I am grateful for:

☐ _____

☐ _____

☐ _____

DAY 97

> *There will always be an opportunity cost. For every opportunity you favor, there is another opportunity you have overlooked. Endeavor to make the right call or it will cost you dearly.*

Today's Three Must Do's:

1. _____

2. _____

3. _____

Today I am grateful for:

☐ _____

☐ _____

☐ _____

DAY 98

> *Follow your dreams today or regret it tomorrow.*

Today's Three Must Do's:

1. _____

2. _____

3. _____

Today I am grateful for:

- [ ] _____
- [ ] _____
- [ ] _____

DAY 99

> *Is your current situation telling you anything? Experience is the best teacher. However, be wise and learn from other people's experiences too.*

Today's Three Must Do's:

1. _____

2. _____

3. _____

Today I am grateful for:

- [ ] _____
- [ ] _____
- [ ] _____

DAY 100

> *No one will write your story better than you. If you are tired of your current story, then start a whole new story on a fresh page, champion!*

Today's Three Must Do's:

1. _____

2. _____

3. _____

Today I am grateful for:

☐ _____

☐ _____

☐ _____

DAY 101

> *Do not be held back by your expectations, society's expectations of you or others' expectations. Remember, holding onto expectations can halt your progress.*

Today's Three Must Do's:

1. _____

2. _____

3. _____

Today I am grateful for:

☐ _____

☐ _____

☐ _____

DAY 102

> *Strive to be early; it will save you the rush.*

Today's Three Must Do's:

1. _____

2. _____

3. _____

Today I am grateful for:

☐ _____

☐ _____

☐ _____

DAY 103

> *Become a believer in your products and what you bring to the table. It is hard to sell what you do not believe in.*

Today's Three Must Do's:

1. _____

2. _____

3. _____

Today I am grateful for:

☐ _____

☐ _____

☐ _____

DAY 104

> *Every day that you are alive, you have another opportunity to dream and to fulfill your purpose.*

Today's Three Must Do's:

1. _____
2. _____
3. _____

Today I am grateful for:

- ☐ _____
- ☐ _____
- ☐ _____

DAY 105

> *Choose not to judge even when you feel strongly that someone is wrong.*

Today's Three Must Do's:

1. _____

2. _____

3. _____

Today I am grateful for:

☐ _____

☐ _____

☐ _____

DAY 106

> *Appreciate and be thankful for the mistakes in life because failure is part of the journey. Failures equip us with lessons and experiences that qualify us.*

Today's Three Must Do's:

1. _____

2. _____

3. _____

Today I am grateful for:

- [ ] _____
- [ ] _____
- [ ] _____

DAY 107

> *In order to go places, you must be intentional. Luck can only take you so far.*

Today's Three Must Do's:

1. _____

2. _____

3. _____

Today I am grateful for:

- ☐ _____
- ☐ _____
- ☐ _____

DAY 108

> *You can sit and wait for situations to become "perfect" forever. Instead, take the first action and improve along the way.*

Today's Three Must Do's:

1. _____

2. _____

3. _____

Today I am grateful for:

☐ _____

☐ _____

☐ _____

DAY 109

> *You have to put in the work and pay it forward because success has a price.*

Today's Three Must Do's:

1. _____

2. _____

3. _____

Today I am grateful for:

☐ _____

☐ _____

☐ _____

DAY 110

> *Always remember that failure is an attribute of the great! Champions fail, dust themselves off and continue until the task finishes. Be a champion.*

Today's Three Must Do's:

1. _____

2. _____

3. _____

Today I am grateful for:

- ☐ _____
- ☐ _____
- ☐ _____

DAY 111

> *How you manage what you cannot control impacts how your life turns out!*

Today's Three Must Do's:

1. _____

2. _____

3. _____

Today I am grateful for:

☐ _____

☐ _____

☐ _____

DAY 112

> *The great miracle lies in accepting and working with what you have.*
>
> *Use what you have in your hand to become the person you see in your head.*

Today's Three Must Do's:

1. _____

2. _____

3. _____

Today I am grateful for:

- [ ] _____
- [ ] _____
- [ ] _____

DAY 113

> *This life is not necessarily about you, but what you do with what is given to you.*

Today's Three Must Do's:

1. _____

2. _____

3. _____

Today I am grateful for:

☐ _____

☐ _____

☐ _____

DAY 114

> *You are created for your own purpose and greatness. Step into it fearlessly.*

Today's Three Must Do's:

1. _____

2. _____

3. _____

Today I am grateful for:

☐ _____

☐ _____

☐ _____

DAY 115

> *Do not get in your way. Instead, take charge of your thoughts and follow up with the respective actions!*

Today's Three Must Do's:

1. _____

2. _____

3. _____

Today I am grateful for:

☐ _____

☐ _____

☐ _____

DAY 116

> *You have everything you need to start pursuing your dream. Remember, other people may not have the same passion you have for your goals and it's ok.*

Today's Three Must Do's:

1. _____

2. _____

3. _____

Today I am grateful for:

☐ _____

☐ _____

☐ _____

DAY 117

> *On the way to success, you must be patient in a world of instant gratification.*

Today's Three Must Do's:

1. _____

2. _____

3. _____

Today I am grateful for:

☐ _____

☐ _____

☐ _____

DAY 118

> *You don't need to know all the answers before you take your first step. However, you will need the first step to see any answer.*

Today's Three Must Do's:

1. _____

2. _____

3. _____

Today I am grateful for:

☐ _____

☐ _____

☐ _____

DAY 119

> *It doesn't take a lot to make a difference. What you don't need could make a difference in someone's life today.*

Today's Three Must Do's:

1. _____

2. _____

3. _____

Today I am grateful for:

☐ _____

☐ _____

☐ _____

DAY 120

> *Be patient and gentle with yourself especially when you fail. Do not write yourself off.*

Today's Three Must Do's:

1. _____

2. _____

3. _____

Today I am grateful for:

☐ _____

☐ _____

☐ _____

DAY 121

> *When you are placed in a position of authority, apply the same rule to everyone including yourself.*

Today's Three Must Do's:

1. _____

2. _____

3. _____

Today I am grateful for:

- [ ] _____
- [ ] _____
- [ ] _____

DAY 122

> *If it feels like your sweat is not yet paying off;*
> *hang in there and try one more time!*

Today's Three Must Do's:

1. _____

2. _____

3. _____

Today I am grateful for:

☐ _____

☐ _____

☐ _____

DAY 123

> *Give yourself permission to step outside of your comfort zone.*

Today's Three Must Do's:

1. _____

2. _____

3. _____

Today I am grateful for:

- [ ] _____
- [ ] _____
- [ ] _____

DAY 124

> *Have a plan B just in case. Don't wait until you get to a roadblock to create a detour.*

Today's Three Must Do's:

1. _____

2. _____

3. _____

Today I am grateful for:

☐ _____

☐ _____

☐ _____

DAY 125

> *You have the power of choice to change your life. And you choose what you let into your life. If you have been making bad decisions, you still have the power to change it. Start by being more thoughtful in your actions.*

Today's Three Must Do's:

1. _____

2. _____

3. _____

Today I am grateful for:

- [ ] _____
- [ ] _____
- [ ] _____

DAY 126

> *You know you are ready for success when you get crystal clear about your life goals and begin motivating yourself.*

Today's Three Must Do's:

1. _____

2. _____

3. _____

Today I am grateful for:

☐ _____

☐ _____

☐ _____

DAY 127

> *Keep it simple. Think of one idea or a problem, solve it and get to the next one. That's how you make a difference.*

Today's Three Must Do's:

1. _____

2. _____

3. _____

Today I am grateful for:

☐ _____

☐ _____

☐ _____

DAY 128

> *Be independent and rely on yourself. Then, you authenticate yourself.*

Today's Three Must Do's:

1. _____

2. _____

3. _____

Today I am grateful for:

☐ _____

☐ _____

☐ _____

DAY 129

> *It is ok not to share every bit of your life with everyone. Keep some secrets. Share what you would like to share at the time you desire to share it.*

Today's Three Must Do's:

1. _____

2. _____

3. _____

Today I am grateful for:

☐ _____

☐ _____

☐ _____

DAY 130

> *Set daily intentions and know what you want to accomplish on a daily basis. Ensure your intentions are visible, so you do not forget them and reduce distractions.*

Today's Three Must Do's:

1. _____

2. _____

3. _____

Today I am grateful for:

☐ _____

☐ _____

☐ _____

DAY 131

> *Use affirmations to counteract negative thinking. Affirm the things you want to see in your life with your mouth.*

Today's Three Must Do's:

1. _____

2. _____

3. _____

Today I am grateful for:

- [ ] _____
- [ ] _____
- [ ] _____

DAY 132

> *Keep sight of the big picture, and press harder using your willpower. Your vision precedes provision.*

Today's Three Must Do's:

1. _____
2. _____
3. _____

Today I am grateful for:

- [ ] _____
- [ ] _____
- [ ] _____

DAY 133

> *Make time for the people you love and the people who love you. Create memories that will last a lifetime.*

Today's Three Must Do's:

1. _____

2. _____

3. _____

Today I am grateful for:

☐ _____

☐ _____

☐ _____

DAY 134

> *What have you done today for your vision? Your vision is your duty alone to pursue — not your family and friends' duty.*

Today's Three Must Do's:

1. _____

2. _____

3. _____

Today I am grateful for:

☐ _____

☐ _____

☐ _____

DAY 135

> *The Internet is not a dumping ground. It is like a party, so get to know people first. Socialize, engage and network. The selling part comes last.*

Today's Three Must Do's:

1. _____

2. _____

3. _____

Today I am grateful for:

☐ _____

☐ _____

☐ _____

DAY 136

> *Discipline will help you build and maintain a routine; seek it and pursue it.*

Today's Three Must Do's:

1. _____

2. _____

3. _____

Today I am grateful for:

☐ _____

☐ _____

☐ _____

DAY 137

> *If you are an entrepreneur, partner with other like-minded entrepreneurs and leverage the power of collaboration. You cannot do it alone.*

Today's Three Must Do's:

1. _____

2. _____

3. _____

Today I am grateful for:

☐ _____

☐ _____

☐ _____

DAY 138

> *When you take a risk, you push boundaries and possibly break barriers. It could be what you need to get to the next level.*

Today's Three Must Do's:

1. _____

2. _____

3. _____

Today I am grateful for:

- ☐ _____
- ☐ _____
- ☐ _____

DAY 139

> *Education may be the only chance for a better life for many people, especially those living in developing countries. Learn and educate yourself with every opportunity.*

Today's Three Must Do's:

1. _____

2. _____

3. _____

Today I am grateful for:

☐ _____

☐ _____

☐ _____

DAY 140

> *Be grateful for where you are. Be thankful for what you have achieved so far, and do not undermine it.*

Today's Three Must Do's:

1. _____
2. _____
3. _____

Today I am grateful for:

☐ _____
☐ _____
☐ _____

DAY 141

> *Be loyal to your goals and do not give up early. Push further lovingly and willingly.*

Today's Three Must Do's:

1. _____

2. _____

3. _____

Today I am grateful for:

☐ _____

☐ _____

☐ _____

DAY 142

> *Always organize and prioritize your tasks and goals. If not, you will be lost in a sea of millions of ideas.*

Today's Three Must Do's:

1. _____

2. _____

3. _____

Today I am grateful for:

☐ _____

☐ _____

☐ _____

DAY 143

> *Be kind even when you are right, always endeavoring to see another's perspective.*

Today's Three Must Do's:

1. _____

2. _____

3. _____

Today I am grateful for:

- [ ] _____
- [ ] _____
- [ ] _____

DAY 144

> *Show optimism regardless of the situation.*

Today's Three Must Do's:

1. _____

2. _____

3. _____

Today I am grateful for:

☐ _____

☐ _____

☐ _____

DAY 145

> *Respect other people's opinion, their religion or lack of it, and equally respect their culture.*

Today's Three Must Do's:

1. _____

2. _____

3. _____

Today I am grateful for:

- [ ] _____
- [ ] _____
- [ ] _____

DAY 146

> *Value people genuinely. Care for your employees if you have employees, and care for your family and friends as well.*

Today's Three Must Do's:

1. _____

2. _____

3. _____

Today I am grateful for:

☐ _____

☐ _____

☐ _____

DAY 147

> *When you have a vision, it becomes easier to create a plan. A vision can also act as a guide through the goal actualization process.*

Today's Three Must Do's:

1. _____

2. _____

3. _____

Today I am grateful for:

☐ _____

☐ _____

☐ _____

DAY 148

> *It's ok to want more from life because that means you are willing to dream more, create more, innovate more and become more. Keep soaring high.*

Today's Three Must Do's:

1. _____

2. _____

3. _____

Today I am grateful for:

☐ _____

☐ _____

☐ _____

DAY 149

> *Learn to show understanding even when the other person shows a total lack of it.*

Today's Three Must Do's:

1. _____

2. _____

3. _____

Today I am grateful for:

☐ _____

☐ _____

☐ _____

DAY 150

> "*See beyond the differences and the asymmetrical components of life. Appreciate the uniqueness and diverseness of life.*"

Today's Three Must Do's:

1. _____

2. _____

3. _____

Today I am grateful for:

- ☐ _____
- ☐ _____
- ☐ _____

DAY 151

> *Don't get sucked into following stories that will not increase the quality of your life. Choose what you let into your life because time is limited.*

Today's Three Must Do's:

1. _____

2. _____

3. _____

Today I am grateful for:

☐ _____

☐ _____

☐ _____

DAY 152

> *You can only start building on what you have by appreciating whatever it is that you have.*

Today's Three Must Do's:

1. _____

2. _____

3. _____

Today I am grateful for:

☐ _____

☐ _____

☐ _____

DAY 153

> *Watch your words and replace your complaints with contentment.*

Today's Three Must Do's:

1. _____

2. _____

3. _____

Today I am grateful for:

☐ _____

☐ _____

☐ _____

DAY 154

> *Be courageous to take up the activities that will move your life forward. Never doubt your ability.*

Today's Three Must Do's:

1. _____

2. _____

3. _____

Today I am grateful for:

☐ _____

☐ _____

☐ _____

DAY 155

> *Remember that your flaws tell stories of your journey. Do not be ashamed of them.*

Today's Three Must Do's:

1. _____

2. _____

3. _____

Today I am grateful for:

- ☐ _____
- ☐ _____
- ☐ _____

DAY 156

> *Be brave and stand up for what you believe in. Don't allow anyone to make you disbelieve your belief.*

Today's Three Must Do's:

1. _____
2. _____
3. _____

Today I am grateful for:

☐ _____
☐ _____
☐ _____

DAY 157

> *Stay focused on your business or mission. If you need to tweak specific strategies, do it. However, do not lose sight of your end goal.*

Today's Three Must Do's:

1. _____

2. _____

3. _____

Today I am grateful for:

☐ _____

☐ _____

☐ _____

DAY 158

> *Today is another beautiful day to write a new page in the story of your life. Make it matter.*

Today's Three Must Do's:

1. _____

2. _____

3. _____

Today I am grateful for:

☐ _____

☐ _____

☐ _____

DAY 159

> *Waiting for the right time is wasting the time you have right now.*

Today's Three Must Do's:

1. _____

2. _____

3. _____

Today I am grateful for:

☐ _____

☐ _____

☐ _____

DAY 160

> *To build a better relationship with family, friends and business partners, choose to treasure and appreciate them rather than ignore and despise them.*

Today's Three Must Do's:

1. _____

2. _____

3. _____

Today I am grateful for:

☐ _____

☐ _____

☐ _____

DAY 161

> *One certain way to win is to spend less time complaining about things you can't change and spend more time concentrating on things that matter.*

Today's Three Must Do's:

1. _____

2. _____

3. _____

Today I am grateful for:

☐ _____

☐ _____

☐ _____

DAY 162

> *Without shifting and taking appropriate action, your situation is not going to change.*

Today's Three Must Do's:

1. _____

2. _____

3. _____

Today I am grateful for:

- ☐ _____
- ☐ _____
- ☐ _____

DAY 163

> *Build a tougher skin to motivate yourself when things get tough. In those situations, you need your strength.*

Today's Three Must Do's:

1. _____

2. _____

3. _____

Today I am grateful for:

☐ _____

☐ _____

☐ _____

DAY 164

> *Self-control and moderation will set you apart because it will protect you from going overboard with things that will distort your plan. Self-control helps hold you accountable as well.*

Today's Three Must Do's:

1. _____
2. _____
3. _____

Today I am grateful for:

- [ ] _____
- [ ] _____
- [ ] _____

DAY 165

> *Validate your ideas by ensuring they are marketable, enduring and bankable.*

Today's Three Must Do's:

1. _____

2. _____

3. _____

Today I am grateful for:

☐ _____

☐ _____

☐ _____

DAY 166

> *Listen to your calling and do not allow fear of the unknown to prevent you from starting.*

Today's Three Must Do's:

1. _____

2. _____

3. _____

Today I am grateful for:

- ☐ _____
- ☐ _____
- ☐ _____

DAY 167

> A leader who appreciates the contribution of his followers and subordinates is more likely to be obeyed, respected, and followed than an arrogant leader who does not value his tribe.

Today's Three Must Do's:

1. _____
2. _____
3. _____

Today I am grateful for:

☐ _____
☐ _____
☐ _____

DAY 168

> *One is many; go for one goal at a time.*
> *Do not overwhelm yourself.*

Today's Three Must Do's:

1. _____

2. _____

3. _____

Today I am grateful for:

☐ _____

☐ _____

☐ _____

DAY 169

> *Do not listen to feelings. Make up your mind on what you need to do and do it.*

Today's Three Must Do's:

1. _____

2. _____

3. _____

Today I am grateful for:

☐ _____

☐ _____

☐ _____

DAY 170

> *Do not be afraid to change up the rules, tweak as you go and follow a routine that works for you.*

Today's Three Must Do's:

1. _____
2. _____
3. _____

Today I am grateful for:

- ☐ _____
- ☐ _____
- ☐ _____

DAY 171

> *If you do not challenge fear, look it in the face and do what you are supposed to do, it will keep you stagnant.*

Today's Three Must Do's:

1. _____

2. _____

3. _____

Today I am grateful for:

☐ _____

☐ _____

☐ _____

DAY 172

> *You don't win a battle by thinking about it or by watching it happen. You win it by taking action and fighting.*

Today's Three Must Do's:

1. _____

2. _____

3. _____

Today I am grateful for:

☐ _____

☐ _____

☐ _____

DAY 173

> *Cultivate a positive mindset. It will help you to maintain a positive outlook towards your circumstances and challenges.*

Today's Three Must Do's:

1. _____

2. _____

3. _____

Today I am grateful for:

☐ _____

☐ _____

☐ _____

DAY 174

> *Do not be afraid to be yourself or share your story. It reveals who you are and the unique experiences you bring to the world.*

Today's Three Must Do's:

1. _____

2. _____

3. _____

Today I am grateful for:

☐ _____

☐ _____

☐ _____

DAY 175

> *If you want to be a great leader, value the people you are leading, respect their opinions, listen and pay attention.*

Today's Three Must Do's:

1. _____

2. _____

3. _____

Today I am grateful for:

- [ ] _____
- [ ] _____
- [ ] _____

DAY 176

> *The will to start and finish any project is in your hands. Put everything you have behind the project and watch how successful it will become.*

Today's Three Must Do's:

1. _____

2. _____

3. _____

Today I am grateful for:

☐ _____

☐ _____

☐ _____

DAY 177

> *You leave a legacy by taking advantage of the opportunities every single day to create something new, memorable and freaking amazing.*

Today's Three Must Do's:

1. _____
2. _____
3. _____

Today I am grateful for:

- ☐ _____
- ☐ _____
- ☐ _____

DAY 178

> *Living your best life involves giving every chosen opportunity your best shot.*

Today's Three Must Do's:

1. _____

2. _____

3. _____

Today I am grateful for:

☐ _____

☐ _____

☐ _____

DAY 179

> *Be patient. Trust the process. As you may have heard many times life is a journey and not a destination.*

Today's Three Must Do's:

1. _____

2. _____

3. _____

Today I am grateful for:

☐ _____

☐ _____

☐ _____

DAY 180

> *Create smaller goals and activities that lead to the completion of your big goal. For instance, if you want to write a book, determine your title first, and then create an outline.*

Today's Three Must Do's:

1. _____

2. _____

3. _____

Today I am grateful for:

☐ _____

☐ _____

☐ _____

DAY 181

> *It is ok to take short breaks in between tasks to recharge, but very long breaks quickly lead to procrastination. Guard against it.*

Today's Three Must Do's:

1. _____

2. _____

3. _____

Today I am grateful for:

☐ _____

☐ _____

☐ _____

DAY 182

> *If you have a message, then think of a platform. A platform gives you an opportunity to serve and be heard.*

Today's Three Must Do's:

1. _____
2. _____
3. _____

Today I am grateful for:

- [ ] _____
- [ ] _____
- [ ] _____

DAY 183

> *When you serve from the heart, you are likely to do your best and develop yourself because every experience has a lesson.*

Today's Three Must Do's:

1. _____

2. _____

3. _____

Today I am grateful for:

☐ _____

☐ _____

☐ _____

DAY 184

> *Don't expect yourself to have all the answers to all the questions you receive; don't pretend to know all the answers either. When in doubt or when you do not know, ask people who know.*

Today's Three Must Do's:

1. _____

2. _____

3. _____

Today I am grateful for:

☐ _____

☐ _____

☐ _____

DAY 185

> *When you collaborate with other like-minded people, it becomes easier to grow and reach more people.*

Today's Three Must Do's:

1. _____

2. _____

3. _____

Today I am grateful for:

☐ _____

☐ _____

☐ _____

DAY 186

> *It is ok to think of a time that you hope to complete a project. But, it is more important to write down that time, and set up the necessary strategy to be accountable to reach your deadline.*

Today's Three Must Do's:

1. _____
2. _____
3. _____

Today I am grateful for:

- ☐ _____
- ☐ _____
- ☐ _____

DAY 187

> *You cannot get better by wishing or by hoping that everything around you will change. You will only get better by sharpening your skills, abilities and improving the things you desire to change.*

Today's Three Must Do's:

1. _____

2. _____

3. _____

Today I am grateful for:

☐ _____

☐ _____

☐ _____

DAY 188

> *It is ok to let go of skills and attitudes that no longer serve you. Don't fret over them.*

Today's Three Must Do's:

1. _____

2. _____

3. _____

Today I am grateful for:

☐ _____

☐ _____

☐ _____

DAY 189

> *Habits are necessary for growth because they will help you keep going even when you run out of a skill set. Nurture new positive habits that will take you to the next level.*

Today's Three Must Do's:

1. _____

2. _____

3. _____

Today I am grateful for:

☐ _____

☐ _____

☐ _____

DAY 190

> *Having a vision is like having a mental picture of where you desire to go. Without a vision, you are wandering around without a purpose.*

Today's Three Must Do's:

1. _____

2. _____

3. _____

Today I am grateful for:

☐ _____

☐ _____

☐ _____

DAY 191

> *Live out your words. People will always believe what you do more than what you say.*

Today's Three Must Do's:

1. _____

2. _____

3. _____

Today I am grateful for:

- [ ] _____
- [ ] _____
- [ ] _____

DAY 192

> *At some point, you've got to take a leap of faith and go for your dream.*

Today's Three Must Do's:

1. _____

2. _____

3. _____

Today I am grateful for:

☐ _____

☐ _____

☐ _____

DAY 193

> *Decide. Do you want this goal or not? There is no time to play around or play yourself.*

Today's Three Must Do's:

1. _____

2. _____

3. _____

Today I am grateful for:

☐ _____

☐ _____

☐ _____

DAY 194

> *There is no entirely new idea on the face of the earth. However, it is essential that your plan has a distinguishable attribute to attract the right people and market.*

Today's Three Must Do's:

1. _____

2. _____

3. _____

Today I am grateful for:

☐ _____

☐ _____

☐ _____

DAY 195

"

Nothing is too small to start from. As long as your goal has your full attention and dedication, you could make it happen with little to no money or resources.

"

Today's Three Must Do's:

1. _____

2. _____

3. _____

Today I am grateful for:

☐ _____

☐ _____

☐ _____

DAY 196

> *If you are a mommy "solo-preneur," it becomes crucial that you remain mindful of your use of time. You could quickly lose yourself in the sea of a gazillion things. And the only time you have to run your business is with the "leftover time," which could adversely affect your growth.*

Today's Three Must Do's:

1. _____
2. _____
3. _____

Today I am grateful for:

☐ _____

☐ _____

☐ _____

DAY 197

> *It is ok to start your business later in life. Better late than never according to the old saying.*

Today's Three Must Do's:

1. _____
2. _____
3. _____

Today I am grateful for:

☐ _____
☐ _____
☐ _____

DAY 198

> *The trials of life are tiresome. The busyness of life is endless. You must brace yourself for the journey of this life, if not, you will be lost in the ride.*

Today's Three Must Do's:

1. _____

2. _____

3. _____

Today I am grateful for:

☐ _____

☐ _____

☐ _____

DAY 199

> *One thing that is constant in life is you. No matter what happens, you will remain at the steering wheel of your life.*

Today's Three Must Do's:

1. _____

2. _____

3. _____

Today I am grateful for:

☐ _____

☐ _____

☐ _____

DAY 200

> *No matter how big your ideas are, you must follow up with actionable steps to become successful. Your actions determine your output.*

Today's Three Must Do's:

1. _____

2. _____

3. _____

Today I am grateful for:

☐ _____

☐ _____

☐ _____

DAY 201

> *There is a bright future for your ideas, but you must develop them to see what that future holds.*

Today's Three Must Do's:

1. _____
2. _____
3. _____

Today I am grateful for:

☐ _____
☐ _____
☐ _____

DAY 202

> *In order for your ideas to become a success story, you must commit to following through with the plan by making it a priority. And you must make your priority your task.*

Today's Three Must Do's:

1. _____

2. _____

3. _____

Today I am grateful for:

☐ _____

☐ _____

☐ _____

DAY 203

"
When you learn from the past, it makes it easier to make sense of the future. It enables you to stand firm in building a solid future foundation.
"

Today's Three Must Do's:

1. _____

2. _____

3. _____

Today I am grateful for:

☐ _____

☐ _____

☐ _____

DAY 204

> *Do not wait for approval anymore. Create your liberty and establish your autonomy.*

Today's Three Must Do's:

1. _____

2. _____

3. _____

Today I am grateful for:

☐ _____

☐ _____

☐ _____

DAY 205

> *Your divine destiny is indestructible. What God has for you is for you, but you must activate it to see its manifestation.*

Today's Three Must Do's:

1. _____

2. _____

3. _____

Today I am grateful for:

☐ _____

☐ _____

☐ _____

DAY 206

> *Position yourself to be stronger than what you have been through. Do not allow the bruises of your past to block the blessings of your future.*

Today's Three Must Do's:

1. _____

2. _____

3. _____

Today I am grateful for:

☐ _____

☐ _____

☐ _____

DAY 207

> *It is never too late to ask for forgiveness when it comes from a genuine heart.*

Today's Three Must Do's:

1. _____

2. _____

3. _____

Today I am grateful for:

☐ _____

☐ _____

☐ _____

DAY 208

> *Life's struggles can make you stronger. Use such strength to your advantage.*

Today's Three Must Do's:

1. _____

2. _____

3. _____

Today I am grateful for:

☐ _____

☐ _____

☐ _____

DAY 209

> *Start turning your life around today. Now is the time to reclaim your blessings; tomorrow may be too late.*

Today's Three Must Do's:

1. _____

2. _____

3. _____

Today I am grateful for:

☐ _____

☐ _____

☐ _____

DAY 210

> *Your opinion is powerful and reveals your belief. Make it matter.*

Today's Three Must Do's:

1. _____

2. _____

3. _____

Today I am grateful for:

☐ _____

☐ _____

☐ _____

DAY 211

> *Do not turn a blind eye to mistreatments going on around you. You could save a life by speaking out.*

Today's Three Must Do's:

1. _____

2. _____

3. _____

Today I am grateful for:

☐ _____

☐ _____

☐ _____

DAY 212

> *Faith is action implemented.*

Today's Three Must Do's:

1. _____

2. _____

3. _____

Today I am grateful for:

☐ _____

☐ _____

☐ _____

DAY 213

> *Move on without hurt and hate. It is worth it.*

Today's Three Must Do's:

1. _____

2. _____

3. _____

Today I am grateful for:

☐ _____

☐ _____

☐ _____

DAY 214

> *Having a vision is not only important, it is a must. It means you at least have an idea of where you are going, and it makes planning easier.*

Today's Three Must Do's:

1. _____

2. _____

3. _____

Today I am grateful for:

☐ _____

☐ _____

☐ _____

DAY 215

> *Today is a day to believe the report of God. You are whole, blessed and fulfilled.*

Today's Three Must Do's:

1. _____

2. _____

3. _____

Today I am grateful for:

☐ _____

☐ _____

☐ _____

DAY 216

> *Remember, in life and business, challenges are inevitable and failure happens. Learn from these opportunities and do not give up.*

Today's Three Must Do's:

1. _____
2. _____
3. _____

Today I am grateful for:

- ☐ _____
- ☐ _____
- ☐ _____

DAY 217

> *Learn to say no sometimes; your success may depend on it.*

Today's Three Must Do's:

1. _____

2. _____

3. _____

Today I am grateful for:

- [ ] _____
- [ ] _____
- [ ] _____

DAY 218

> *Know and appreciate your worth. Knowing who you are means acknowledging what you bring to the table.*

Today's Three Must Do's:

1. _____

2. _____

3. _____

Today I am grateful for:

☐ _____

☐ _____

☐ _____

DAY 219

> *To get ahead, you must take care of your health.*

Today's Three Must Do's:

1. _____

2. _____

3. _____

Today I am grateful for:

☐ _____

☐ _____

☐ _____

DAY 220

> *Beware of how you treat other people especially when you are on your way up. Be kind to others and it will come back to you..*

Today's Three Must Do's:

1. _____

2. _____

3. _____

Today I am grateful for:

☐ _____

☐ _____

☐ _____

DAY 221

> *Be compassionate with yourself and forgive yourself, then you can show the same to other people who need it.*

Today's Three Must Do's:

1. _____

2. _____

3. _____

Today I am grateful for:

☐ _____

☐ _____

☐ _____

DAY 222

> *Do not be afraid to learn, unlearn and re-learn. It is an integral part of getting ahead in life.*

Today's Three Must Do's:

1. _____
2. _____
3. _____

Today I am grateful for:

☐ _____
☐ _____
☐ _____

DAY 223

> *No matter who is right or wrong during a disagreement, be willing to show respect. It will take you far.*

Today's Three Must Do's:

1. _____

2. _____

3. _____

Today I am grateful for:

☐ _____

☐ _____

☐ _____

DAY 224

> *Go the extra mile; you will thank yourself later. If you have been asked to run one mile, run two. If you have been asked to eat a plate of salad once a week, make it three.*

Today's Three Must Do's:

1. _____

2. _____

3. _____

Today I am grateful for:

☐ _____

☐ _____

☐ _____

DAY 225

> *When you show up prepared consistently, one day you will have a miracle.*

Today's Three Must Do's:

1. _____

2. _____

3. _____

Today I am grateful for:

☐ _____

☐ _____

☐ _____

DAY 226

> *Some strategies work better than others. Do more of what works and less of what doesn't.*

Today's Three Must Do's:

1. _____

2. _____

3. _____

Today I am grateful for:

☐ _____

☐ _____

☐ _____

DAY 227

> *Make up your mind to stop procrastinating. Nothing gets done unless you do it.*

Today's Three Must Do's:

1. _____

2. _____

3. _____

Today I am grateful for:

☐ _____

☐ _____

☐ _____

DAY 228

> *You need to be happy in order to become successful. But, you don't need to be successful to experience happiness.*

Today's Three Must Do's:

1. _____

2. _____

3. _____

Today I am grateful for:

☐ _____

☐ _____

☐ _____

DAY 229

> *If you live in a country where freedom of choice exists, be thankful. Many people in different parts of the world don't.*

Today's Three Must Do's:

1. _____
2. _____
3. _____

Today I am grateful for:

☐ _____

☐ _____

☐ _____

DAY 230

> The only way to guarantee a better tomorrow is by working hard today. Put your best foot forward in your business or priorities so you can secure a better result in the future.

Today's Three Must Do's:

1. _____

2. _____

3. _____

Today I am grateful for:

☐ _____

☐ _____

☐ _____

DAY 231

> *Work on your vision now. Don't wait on it. The right time to manifest it is now.*

Today's Three Must Do's:

1. _____

2. _____

3. _____

Today I am grateful for:

☐ _____

☐ _____

☐ _____

DAY 232

> *Do not get too comfortable with your current status that you forget to pursue your dreams.*

Today's Three Must Do's:

1. _____

2. _____

3. _____

Today I am grateful for:

☐ _____

☐ _____

☐ _____

DAY 233

> *Life is not built on fairytale. In life, you get what you work for.*

Today's Three Must Do's:

1. _____

2. _____

3. _____

Today I am grateful for:

- [ ] _____
- [ ] _____
- [ ] _____

DAY 234

> *You are not alone in the daily struggles and temptation to quit, so don't take it personally. Keep your head up and keep pushing.*

Today's Three Must Do's:

1. _____

2. _____

3. _____

Today I am grateful for:

☐ _____

☐ _____

☐ _____

DAY 235

> *Today, start acting on your goals by defining the purpose of those goals.*

Today's Three Must Do's:

1. _____

2. _____

3. _____

Today I am grateful for:

☐ _____

☐ _____

☐ _____

DAY 236

> *Be on top of your game. Make a personal assessment of where you are because it will set a tone for where you desire to go.*

Today's Three Must Do's:

1. _____

2. _____

3. _____

Today I am grateful for:

☐ _____

☐ _____

☐ _____

DAY 237

> *Start creating healthy and helpful habits like waking up early. Good habits enhance productivity.*

Today's Three Must Do's:

1. _____

2. _____

3. _____

Today I am grateful for:

☐ _____

☐ _____

☐ _____

DAY 238

> *Ask questions! Don't pretend to know what you do not know. A question can save your life or business.*

Today's Three Must Do's:

1. _____

2. _____

3. _____

Today I am grateful for:

☐ _____

☐ _____

☐ _____

DAY 239

> *Today, don't wish, work. The simplest and smartest way for anyone to achieve success is for that person to work on their goals and nothing else.*

Today's Three Must Do's:

1. _____

2. _____

3. _____

Today I am grateful for:

☐ _____

☐ _____

☐ _____

DAY 240

> *Be grateful every single day. Gratitude helps you appreciate the value you bring to yourself and others.*

Today's Three Must Do's:

1. _____

2. _____

3. _____

Today I am grateful for:

☐ _____

☐ _____

☐ _____

DAY 241

> *Intentional actions are the only way to reach your goal.*

Today's Three Must Do's:

1. _____

2. _____

3. _____

Today I am grateful for:

☐ _____

☐ _____

☐ _____

DAY 242

> *Anyone can come up with an excuse. Eventually, excuses don't get you anywhere. It makes you unreliable, untrustworthy and irresponsible.*

Today's Three Must Do's:

1. _____

2. _____

3. _____

Today I am grateful for:

☐ _____

☐ _____

☐ _____

DAY 243

> *When in doubt, get an accountability partner. They can help you stay focused on your priority.*

Today's Three Must Do's:

1. _____

2. _____

3. _____

Today I am grateful for:

☐ _____

☐ _____

☐ _____

DAY 244

> *Certain decisions may require swift action, act swiftly on those. Don't delay or sleep on them. It could cost you.*

Today's Three Must Do's:

1. _____

2. _____

3. _____

Today I am grateful for:

☐ _____

☐ _____

☐ _____

DAY 245

> *Do not make every task a priority because they are not. Instead, make your priority your responsibility.*

Today's Three Must Do's:

1. _____

2. _____

3. _____

Today I am grateful for:

☐ _____

☐ _____

☐ _____

DAY 246

> *At the end of the day, remind yourself of your most significant achievements. Always appreciate the struggle.*

Today's Three Must Do's:

1. _____

2. _____

3. _____

Today I am grateful for:

☐ _____

☐ _____

☐ _____

DAY 247

> *Practice to become better in whatever area of talent you currently have.*

Today's Three Must Do's:

1. _____

2. _____

3. _____

Today I am grateful for:

☐ _____

☐ _____

☐ _____

DAY 248

> *Do not become dependent on anything including your gadgets. The only thing you can depend on is God and yourself.*

Today's Three Must Do's:

1. _____

2. _____

3. _____

Today I am grateful for:

☐ _____

☐ _____

☐ _____

DAY 249

> *Don't wait. While waiting, do something instead. Time wasted will never be recovered.*

Today's Three Must Do's:

1. _____

2. _____

3. _____

Today I am grateful for:

☐ _____

☐ _____

☐ _____

DAY 250

> *This time go from start to finish on the goal. Do not abandon your project halfway.*

Today's Three Must Do's:

1. _____

2. _____

3. _____

Today I am grateful for:

☐ _____

☐ _____

☐ _____

DAY 251

> *Do not entertain the noise because you want to belong. Nothing is worth losing your peace.*

Today's Three Must Do's:

1. _____

2. _____

3. _____

Today I am grateful for:

☐ _____

☐ _____

☐ _____

DAY 252

> *Review your tasks routinely. You are better off completing them promptly.*

Today's Three Must Do's:

1. _____

2. _____

3. _____

Today I am grateful for:

- [ ] _____
- [ ] _____
- [ ] _____

DAY 253

> *Do your high priority tasks during your most productive time.*

Today's Three Must Do's:

1. _____

2. _____

3. _____

Today I am grateful for:

☐ _____

☐ _____

☐ _____

DAY 254

> *Do not cover up your insufficiency and failures, instead work to improve them.*

Today's Three Must Do's:

1. _____

2. _____

3. _____

Today I am grateful for:

☐ _____

☐ _____

☐ _____

DAY 255

> *No matter how crazy life gets, don't forget how awesome you are.*

Today's Three Must Do's:

1. _____

2. _____

3. _____

Today I am grateful for:

- [ ] _____
- [ ] _____
- [ ] _____

DAY 256

> *Practice getting up on time. It enables you to have more time to yourself.*

Today's Three Must Do's:

1. _____

2. _____

3. _____

Today I am grateful for:

- ☐ _____
- ☐ _____
- ☐ _____

DAY 257

> *There is more to life than existing. Tap into your abundance of knowledge and make more out of life.*

Today's Three Must Do's:

1. _____
2. _____
3. _____

Today I am grateful for:

☐ _____
☐ _____
☐ _____

DAY 258

> *Being alive is a blessing. Staying alive is a hustle. And living your life according to your own terms is a treasure.*

Today's Three Must Do's:

1. _____

2. _____

3. _____

Today I am grateful for:

☐ _____

☐ _____

☐ _____

DAY 259

> *Do not be held back by your past thoughts, present thoughts or future thoughts. Set yourself free from the ideas that hold you hostage.*

Today's Three Must Do's:

1. _____

2. _____

3. _____

Today I am grateful for:

☐ _____

☐ _____

☐ _____

DAY 260

> *Be brave and use your gifts today and not tomorrow, for tomorrow is not promised.*

Today's Three Must Do's:

1. _____

2. _____

3. _____

Today I am grateful for:

☐ _____

☐ _____

☐ _____

DAY 261

> *Do not be afraid of the big leaps. They could be what you need for your next level.*

Today's Three Must Do's:

1. _____

2. _____

3. _____

Today I am grateful for:

☐ _____

☐ _____

☐ _____

DAY 262

> *How you are living your life today not tomorrow is what matters. The work you put in today creates the gain you will enjoy tomorrow.*

Today's Three Must Do's:

1. _____

2. _____

3. _____

Today I am grateful for:

☐ _____

☐ _____

☐ _____

DAY 263

> *It is important that you quit sitting on the fence and take a side. Begin to take action today.*

Today's Three Must Do's:

1. _____
2. _____
3. _____

Today I am grateful for:

☐ _____
☐ _____
☐ _____

DAY 264

> *If you are not willing to get laser-focused on your next cause of action, you are not ready to grow.*

Today's Three Must Do's:

1. _____

2. _____

3. _____

Today I am grateful for:

☐ _____

☐ _____

☐ _____

DAY 265

> *You are the only one who can decide to take back your life. When you are ready, tell yourself that "enough is enough."*

Today's Three Must Do's:

1. _____

2. _____

3. _____

Today I am grateful for:

☐ _____

☐ _____

☐ _____

DAY 267

> *I have the power to begin where I am.*

Today's Three Must Do's:

1. _____

2. _____

3. _____

Today I am grateful for:

- ☐ _____
- ☐ _____
- ☐ _____

DAY 268

> *When you realize that tomorrow is not promised, it becomes even more imperative that you wake up from slumber.*

Today's Three Must Do's:

1. _____

2. _____

3. _____

Today I am grateful for:

☐ _____

☐ _____

☐ _____

DAY 269

> *Step up, and the world will catch up.*

Today's Three Must Do's:

1. _____

2. _____

3. _____

Today I am grateful for:

☐ _____

☐ _____

☐ _____

DAY 270

> *We are human. We are not without faults. Do not beat yourself down when your performance is not up to par.*

Today's Three Must Do's:

1. _____

2. _____

3. _____

Today I am grateful for:

☐ _____

☐ _____

☐ _____

DAY 271

> *When everything becomes a priority, nothing is a priority.*

Today's Three Must Do's:

1. _____

2. _____

3. _____

Today I am grateful for:

☐ _____

☐ _____

☐ _____

DAY 272

> *You are created for your own purpose and greatness. Do not wait for other people to lead you to your life's manifestation. You must lead the way.*

Today's Three Must Do's:

1. _____

2. _____

3. _____

Today I am grateful for:

☐ _____

☐ _____

☐ _____

DAY 273

> *Guess what? If you start walking faster, people who want to walk with you will catch up.*

Today's Three Must Do's:

1. _____

2. _____

3. _____

Today I am grateful for:

☐ _____

☐ _____

☐ _____

DAY 274

> *Forgiveness is one of the simplest, yet most powerful, ways to set the tone for your life.*

Today's Three Must Do's:

1. _____

2. _____

3. _____

Today I am grateful for:

☐ _____

☐ _____

☐ _____

DAY 275

> *The moment you realize that you cannot be everything to everybody is the moment you start living and stop existing.*

Today's Three Must Do's:

1. _____

2. _____

3. _____

Today I am grateful for:

☐ _____

☐ _____

☐ _____

DAY 276

> *Stop living like a cat with nine lives; you have only one. Life has no duplicate.*

Today's Three Must Do's:

1. _____

2. _____

3. _____

Today I am grateful for:

- [ ] _____
- [ ] _____
- [ ] _____

DAY 277

> *You have the power to make the right decisions about your situation every single time.*

Today's Three Must Do's:

1. _____

2. _____

3. _____

Today I am grateful for:

☐ _____

☐ _____

☐ _____

DAY 278

> *Today, I will think for myself and take appropriate actions that align with my intentions.*

Today's Three Must Do's:

1. _____

2. _____

3. _____

Today I am grateful for:

☐ _____

☐ _____

☐ _____

DAY 279

> *You have to control your time during the day. If not, your day will dictate what happens to you.*

Today's Three Must Do's:

1. _____

2. _____

3. _____

Today I am grateful for:

☐ _____

☐ _____

☐ _____

DAY 280

> *If you really understand that you have one shot at life, then give yourself the permission and freedom to dream and execute those goals that will both excite and scare you.*

Today's Three Must Do's:

1. _____

2. _____

3. _____

Today I am grateful for:

☐ _____

☐ _____

☐ _____

DAY 281

> *Kindness will never run out of fashion; show and share some today.*

Today's Three Must Do's:

1. _____

2. _____

3. _____

Today I am grateful for:

☐ _____

☐ _____

☐ _____

DAY 282

> *If you ever want to get to where you are going, it is highly critical that you value your time.*

Today's Three Must Do's:

1. _____

2. _____

3. _____

Today I am grateful for:

☐ _____

☐ _____

☐ _____

DAY 283

> *What matters in your matter is your opinion, that's all.*

Today's Three Must Do's:

1. _____

2. _____

3. _____

Today I am grateful for:

- [ ] _____
- [ ] _____
- [ ] _____

DAY 284

> *Don't ever think that you are alone, that the world has forsaken you, or that your troubles are the worst. There is always someone somewhere having it worse.*

Today's Three Must Do's:

1. _____

2. _____

3. _____

Today I am grateful for:

☐ _____

☐ _____

☐ _____

DAY 285

> *When you compete with yourself, it helps you get better. When you fight with other people around you, it leads to resentment and unhealthy rivalries.*

Today's Three Must Do's:

1. _____
2. _____
3. _____

Today I am grateful for:

- [ ] _____
- [ ] _____
- [ ] _____

DAY 286

> *Everyone is running a separate race in this lifetime.*

Today's Three Must Do's:

1. _____

2. _____

3. _____

Today I am grateful for:

- [ ] _____
- [ ] _____
- [ ] _____

DAY 287

> *Any time is a great time to start taking actions toward the goals that you desire to accomplish but the earlier, the better.*

Today's Three Must Do's:

1. _____
2. _____
3. _____

Today I am grateful for:

- [ ] _____
- [ ] _____
- [ ] _____

DAY 288

> When you maintain a high level of authenticity in things you do, you will marvel at your result. Most times people buy into you before they buy from you.

Today's Three Must Do's:

1. _____

2. _____

3. _____

Today I am grateful for:

☐ _____

☐ _____

☐ _____

DAY 289

> *Focus on your interest, embrace it and give it an opportunity to shine.*

Today's Three Must Do's:

1. _____

2. _____

3. _____

Today I am grateful for:

☐ _____

☐ _____

☐ _____

DAY 290

> *Change starts from what you think about and how you think about it.*

Today's Three Must Do's:

1. _____

2. _____

3. _____

Today I am grateful for:

- [ ] _____
- [ ] _____
- [ ] _____

DAY 291

> *The only opinion that really matters is your opinion, your opinions about your situation and circumstances, and your opinion about your visions, dreams, and goals.*

Today's Three Must Do's:

1. _____

2. _____

3. _____

Today I am grateful for:

☐ _____

☐ _____

☐ _____

DAY 292

> *There are many opportunities that you miss every day when you do not show up.*

Today's Three Must Do's:

1. _____

2. _____

3. _____

Today I am grateful for:

☐ _____

☐ _____

☐ _____

DAY 293

> *In life, how you start doesn't necessarily equal how you end. But, in order to end well, you must continually show up.*

Today's Three Must Do's:

1. _____

2. _____

3. _____

Today I am grateful for:

☐ _____

☐ _____

☐ _____

DAY 294

> *The most reasonable thing to do is to outsmart time. When you plan and act ahead, you don't have to play catch up.*

Today's Three Must Do's:

1. _____

2. _____

3. _____

Today I am grateful for:

- [ ] _____
- [ ] _____
- [ ] _____

DAY 295

> *Failing in one area doesn't mean failing in all areas. However, failure shows that you now have experience in the area you have failed.*

Today's Three Must Do's:

1. _____

2. _____

3. _____

Today I am grateful for:

- ☐ _____
- ☐ _____
- ☐ _____

DAY 296

> *Find a way to make what you have work for you. Start and inspiration will come.*

Today's Three Must Do's:

1. _____

2. _____

3. _____

Today I am grateful for:

- [ ] _____
- [ ] _____
- [ ] _____

DAY 297

> *Your situation is not beyond your capability.*

Today's Three Must Do's:

1. _____

2. _____

3. _____

Today I am grateful for:

☐ _____

☐ _____

☐ _____

DAY 298

> *See beyond your problems and be ready to push until there are no more walls blocking you from your destiny.*

Today's Three Must Do's:

1. _____

2. _____

3. _____

Today I am grateful for:

☐ _____

☐ _____

☐ _____

DAY 299

> *Some opinions may be valid, logical or a genuine concern. However, you still have the final say regarding your situation, which you know better than anyone else.*

Today's Three Must Do's:

1. _____

2. _____

3. _____

Today I am grateful for:

☐ _____

☐ _____

☐ _____

DAY 300

> *What you commit yourself to do is what you think about. And what you think about is what you achieve.*

Today's Three Must Do's:

1. _____

2. _____

3. _____

Today I am grateful for:

- [ ] _____
- [ ] _____
- [ ] _____

DAY 301

> *Having hope helps you see the light at the end of the tunnel even if it is dark.*

Today's Three Must Do's:

1. _____

2. _____

3. _____

Today I am grateful for:

☐ _____

☐ _____

☐ _____

DAY 302

> *Your choice takes you closer or farther away from your vision. Thus, your choice is key to your success.*

Today's Three Must Do's:

1. _____

2. _____

3. _____

Today I am grateful for:

- [ ] _____
- [ ] _____
- [ ] _____

DAY 303

> *Do not be afraid to say no to situations and circumstances that will take away your peace. Nurture and protect your peace.*

Today's Three Must Do's:

1. _____

2. _____

3. _____

Today I am grateful for:

☐ _____

☐ _____

☐ _____

DAY 304

"

It is easy to see all that you do not have or cannot afford; look beyond and believe to receive.

"

Today's Three Must Do's:

1. _____

2. _____

3. _____

Today I am grateful for:

☐ _____

☐ _____

☐ _____

DAY 305

> *The poverty of the mind can keep you from using your intelligence. And you could find yourself stuck when you should be on the move.*

Today's Three Must Do's:

1. _____

2. _____

3. _____

Today I am grateful for:

☐ _____

☐ _____

☐ _____

DAY 306

> *How can you have enough if you are not enough in your own eyes? Begin to realize your worth so you can use your wings.*

Today's Three Must Do's:

1. _____

2. _____

3. _____

Today I am grateful for:

☐ _____

☐ _____

☐ _____

DAY 307

> *Success is the result of hard work not "head work." Though "head work" is part of it because you conceptualize your ideas in your head. But, you must go from formation to finish to see physical manifestation.*

Today's Three Must Do's:

1. _____
2. _____
3. _____

Today I am grateful for:

- ☐ _____
- ☐ _____
- ☐ _____

DAY 308

> *In becoming the person you want to be, it is important to know that you have the power to be that incredible person you envision.*

Today's Three Must Do's:

1. _____

2. _____

3. _____

Today I am grateful for:

☐ _____

☐ _____

☐ _____

DAY 309

> *Every dream can be delivered. Every idea can be innovated. Everything is possible if we are committed.*

Today's Three Must Do's:

1. _____

2. _____

3. _____

Today I am grateful for:

☐ _____

☐ _____

☐ _____

DAY 310

> *Actions are the lifeline of dream demonstration.*

Today's Three Must Do's:

1. _____

2. _____

3. _____

Today I am grateful for:

☐ _____

☐ _____

☐ _____

DAY 311

> *Be grateful in the moment of struggle when your strength is fortified, and your perseverance is proved.*

Today's Three Must Do's:

1. _____
2. _____
3. _____

Today I am grateful for:

- [ ] _____
- [ ] _____
- [ ] _____

DAY 312

> *At the end of your journey on this earth, there will be no one to blame but you for any unaccomplished goal or unlived life.*

Today's Three Must Do's:

1. _____

2. _____

3. _____

Today I am grateful for:

☐ _____

☐ _____

☐ _____

DAY 313

> *Changing your life largely depends on your attention and action.*

Today's Three Must Do's:

1. _____

2. _____

3. _____

Today I am grateful for:

☐ _____

☐ _____

☐ _____

DAY 314

> *Become the champion of your greatness.*

Today's Three Must Do's:

1. _____

2. _____

3. _____

Today I am grateful for:

☐ _____

☐ _____

☐ _____

DAY 315

> *The only way for you to reach your goal is for you to start, stay on course, and complete the course.*

Today's Three Must Do's:

1. _____

2. _____

3. _____

Today I am grateful for:

☐ _____

☐ _____

☐ _____

DAY 316

> *Whoever you end up becoming has a lot to do with your mindset not your background.*

Today's Three Must Do's:

1. _____

2. _____

3. _____

Today I am grateful for:

- [ ] _____
- [ ] _____
- [ ] _____

DAY 317

> *Have hope that something good will happen at the end of the day because when you lose hope you start losing everything.*

Today's Three Must Do's:

1. _____

2. _____

3. _____

Today I am grateful for:

☐ _____

☐ _____

☐ _____

DAY 318

> *Begin to speak with your mouth whatever you would like to see happen in your life and begin to act in that manner too.*

Today's Three Must Do's:

1. _____

2. _____

3. _____

Today I am grateful for:

- [ ] _____
- [ ] _____
- [ ] _____

DAY 319

> *The seasons of life are architects of hope.*

Today's Three Must Do's:

1. _____

2. _____

3. _____

Today I am grateful for:

- ☐ _____
- ☐ _____
- ☐ _____

DAY 320

> *Conquering poverty will never happen by sheer luck or chance, but by a change of mindset, hard work, determination, perseverance, opportunity creation, hope, and tenacity all built on a solid foundation of equality and abundance thinking.*

Today's Three Must Do's:

1. _____

2. _____

3. _____

Today I am grateful for:

☐ _____

☐ _____

☐ _____

DAY 321

> *Changes create golden chances, but you still must choose to allow it.*

Today's Three Must Do's:

1. _____

2. _____

3. _____

Today I am grateful for:

☐ _____

☐ _____

☐ _____

DAY 322

> *The way out of poverty could become a matter of life and death. So, you must be all in.*

Today's Three Must Do's:

1. _____

2. _____

3. _____

Today I am grateful for:

☐ _____

☐ _____

☐ _____

DAY 323

> *Do not sacrifice long-term glory for short-term gain.*

Today's Three Must Do's:

1. _____

2. _____

3. _____

Today I am grateful for:

☐ _____

☐ _____

☐ _____

DAY 324

> *A seed will never have an opportunity to develop if it was never planted.*

Today's Three Must Do's:

1. _____

2. _____

3. _____

Today I am grateful for:

☐ _____

☐ _____

☐ _____

DAY 325

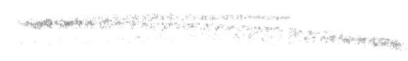

"
Be willing to question what you consume and give your time and attention to.
"

Today's Three Must Do's:

1. _____

2. _____

3. _____

Today I am grateful for:

☐ _____

☐ _____

☐ _____

DAY 326

> *Everything that happened previously offers an opportunity for healing, progress and growth.*

Today's Three Must Do's:

1. _____
2. _____
3. _____

Today I am grateful for:

☐ _____

☐ _____

☐ _____

DAY 327

> *Put your energy behind your talent and make your talent extraordinary.*

Today's Three Must Do's:

1. _____

2. _____

3. _____

Today I am grateful for:

- [ ] _____
- [ ] _____
- [ ] _____

DAY 328

> *If, in any way, shape or form you do not like your life situations, change them; start walking in the direction of what you want to be.*

Today's Three Must Do's:

1. _____

2. _____

3. _____

Today I am grateful for:

☐ _____

☐ _____

☐ _____

DAY 329

> *The will to accomplish anything is already within you, but you will need to start using your will to improve your life.*

Today's Three Must Do's:

1. _____

2. _____

3. _____

Today I am grateful for:

☐ _____

☐ _____

☐ _____

DAY 330

> *The truth is that when you are working with limited resources like land, time, and energy, you must be intentional because they don't have duplicates.*

Today's Three Must Do's:

1. _____
2. _____
3. _____

Today I am grateful for:

- ☐ _____
- ☐ _____
- ☐ _____

DAY 331

> *Do not allow anger to overrule your good judgment.*

Today's Three Must Do's:

1. _____

2. _____

3. _____

Today I am grateful for:

☐ _____

☐ _____

☐ _____

DAY 332

> *Have your best interest at heart at all times. Show compassion to yourself and then to others.*

Today's Three Must Do's:

1. _____

2. _____

3. _____

Today I am grateful for:

☐ _____

☐ _____

☐ _____

DAY 333

> *Live by what you profess because behaviors are best taught by modeling.*

Today's Three Must Do's:

1. _____

2. _____

3. _____

Today I am grateful for:

☐ _____

☐ _____

☐ _____

DAY 334

> *It will be hard to tell someone who cannot afford a meal to save for college because the immediate need of that person is food.*

Today's Three Must Do's:

1. _____

2. _____

3. _____

Today I am grateful for:

☐ _____

☐ _____

☐ _____

DAY 335

> *A dream and talk alone can only go so far — you must build. You must work with your hands to deliver your goals and vision.*

Today's Three Must Do's:

1. _____

2. _____

3. _____

Today I am grateful for:

☐ _____

☐ _____

☐ _____

DAY 336

> *Be grateful. Gratitude brings your blessings and miracles closer than you will ever know or imagine.*

Today's Three Must Do's:

1. _____

2. _____

3. _____

Today I am grateful for:

- ☐ _____
- ☐ _____
- ☐ _____

DAY 337

> *Forgive. An unforgiving spirit can diminish your shine, reduce progress and halt advancement.*

Today's Three Must Do's:

1. _____
2. _____
3. _____

Today I am grateful for:

- ☐ _____
- ☐ _____
- ☐ _____

DAY 338

> *We don't have control over certain things, such as how we come into this world or how we start some journeys. But as you become of age, you can start rewriting your story.*

Today's Three Must Do's:

1. _____
2. _____
3. _____

Today I am grateful for:

☐ _____
☐ _____
☐ _____

DAY 339

> *Your determination is demonstrated at the time of defeat.*

Today's Three Must Do's:

1. _____

2. _____

3. _____

Today I am grateful for:

☐ _____

☐ _____

☐ _____

DAY 340

> *Today, decide to be the hero in your life; start and don't look back.*

Today's Three Must Do's:

1. _____

2. _____

3. _____

Today I am grateful for:

☐ _____

☐ _____

☐ _____

DAY 341

> *Quit supporting situations that are not growing your life.*

Today's Three Must Do's:

1. _____

2. _____

3. _____

Today I am grateful for:

☐ _____

☐ _____

☐ _____

DAY 342

> *Do not be too busy to show appreciation for exceptional deeds done and blessings in your life.*

Today's Three Must Do's:

1. _____

2. _____

3. _____

Today I am grateful for:

☐ _____

☐ _____

☐ _____

DAY 343

> *You can never outgrow "doing the work." No matter how far you have come, you will still get better by practicing.*

Today's Three Must Do's:

1. _____

2. _____

3. _____

Today I am grateful for:

☐ _____

☐ _____

☐ _____

DAY 344

> *Failing in one area doesn't mean failing in all areas. Do not be afraid to try a new skill or business venture.*

Today's Three Must Do's:

1. _____

2. _____

3. _____

Today I am grateful for:

☐ _____

☐ _____

☐ _____

DAY 345

> *Run your business like a business and not like a charity. Set boundaries between personal inclinations and business ventures.*

Today's Three Must Do's:

1. _____

2. _____

3. _____

Today I am grateful for:

- [ ] _____
- [ ] _____
- [ ] _____

DAY 346

> *Do not underrate the hard work that your success requires. Go above and beyond. Stretch yourself and become who you have been created to be.*

Today's Three Must Do's:

1. _____

2. _____

3. _____

Today I am grateful for:

☐ _____

☐ _____

☐ _____

DAY 347

> *The world today is challenging enough. Do not let negative people make it even worse. You deserve better.*

Today's Three Must Do's:

1. _____

2. _____

3. _____

Today I am grateful for:

☐ _____

☐ _____

☐ _____

DAY 348

> *Time is one of your most expensive assets; protect it with all you have.*

Today's Three Must Do's:

1. _____

2. _____

3. _____

Today I am grateful for:

- [ ] _____
- [ ] _____
- [ ] _____

DAY 349

> *The power to make your own choice is the ultimate power to succeed in life.*

Today's Three Must Do's:

1. _____

2. _____

3. _____

Today I am grateful for:

☐ _____

☐ _____

☐ _____

DAY 350

> *Can people take advantage of your kindness? YES! But should you and I allow those terrible experiences to stop us from showing compassion? NOPE!*

Today's Three Must Do's:

1. _____

2. _____

3. _____

Today I am grateful for:

☐ _____

☐ _____

☐ _____

DAY 351

> *When you let your responsibility slide away, and you blame it on your environment and DNA, you are losing a grip on your life.*

Today's Three Must Do's:

1. _____

2. _____

3. _____

Today I am grateful for:

☐ _____

☐ _____

☐ _____

DAY 352

> *Look beyond your challenges. Look into those small opportunities and make wise decisions that your success journey requires.*

Today's Three Must Do's:

1. _____

2. _____

3. _____

Today I am grateful for:

☐ _____

☐ _____

☐ _____

DAY 353

> *Accountability is one of the ways you can stop your environment from controlling your destiny.*

Today's Three Must Do's:

1. _____

2. _____

3. _____

Today I am grateful for:

- ☐ _____
- ☐ _____
- ☐ _____

DAY 354

"

Money and status may sometimes give you pleasure and satisfaction, but such happiness is always short-lived. Instead, seek the joy that comes from within.

"

Today's Three Must Do's:

1. _____

2. _____

3. _____

Today I am grateful for:

☐ _____

☐ _____

☐ _____

DAY 355

> *Growth would never happen without struggles because it is part of the process. Therefore, see every growing battle as a grateful experience.*

Today's Three Must Do's:

1. _____
2. _____
3. _____

Today I am grateful for:

- [ ] _____
- [ ] _____
- [ ] _____

DAY 356

> *There will always be something going on, but is it meant for you or your consumption?*

Today's Three Must Do's:

1. _____

2. _____

3. _____

Today I am grateful for:

☐ _____

☐ _____

☐ _____

DAY 357

> *Plan your day the night before; nothing happens by accident.*

Today's Three Must Do's:

1. _____

2. _____

3. _____

Today I am grateful for:

☐ _____

☐ _____

☐ _____

DAY 358

> Growth requires food. Feed on excellent foods that will nourish your body, soul, and output.

Today's Three Must Do's:

1. _____

2. _____

3. _____

Today I am grateful for:

- [ ] _____
- [ ] _____
- [ ] _____

DAY 359

> *Learn not to blame your circumstances when things go wrong, accept responsibility, learn from them and move on.*

Today's Three Must Do's:

1. _____

2. _____

3. _____

Today I am grateful for:

- [ ] _____
- [ ] _____
- [ ] _____

DAY 360

> *Because there is a limit to the amount of time we have in a day and the length of life we live on this earth, it is important you start now rather than later.*

Today's Three Must Do's:

1. _____

2. _____

3. _____

Today I am grateful for:

☐ _____

☐ _____

☐ _____

DAY 361

> *Be attentive to character, listen to cues, and do not be deceived by word of mouth; action will always reveal the right identity.*

Today's Three Must Do's:

1. _____

2. _____

3. _____

Today I am grateful for:

☐ _____

☐ _____

☐ _____

DAY 362

> *The big things are reminders that everything is possible. The small things are reminders that everything is beautiful and that every moment is important.*

Today's Three Must Do's:

1. _____

2. _____

3. _____

Today I am grateful for:

☐ _____

☐ _____

☐ _____

DAY 363

> *Everything may not be perfect and exactly where you want it to be from the beginning, but you must start with faith.*

Today's Three Must Do's:

1. _____

2. _____

3. _____

Today I am grateful for:

- ☐ _____
- ☐ _____
- ☐ _____

DAY 364

> *If you desire to grow your trade, you must practice your trade. No one can become an expert in a business he or she knows nothing about.*

Today's Three Must Do's:

1. _____

2. _____

3. _____

Today I am grateful for:

☐ _____

☐ _____

☐ _____

DAY 365

> "
> *The key to not allowing others to take advantage of your good heart is by setting boundaries and understanding that you can never please everyone.*
> "

Today's Three Must Do's:

1. _____

2. _____

3. _____

Today I am grateful for:

☐ _____

☐ _____

☐ _____

ACKNOWLEDGMENTS

A round of applause to my family: Kemka, Kamsi, and Mich. Thanks for your support and love. Thanks for understanding or at least pretending to understand "when mommy is still working at her desk" after working hours. Thanks for your patience.

Thanks to the Periscope TV team. In March 2018, I received the highest periscope VIP status – the gold badge, a clear indication that intentional daily action does indeed pay off. I have also received tremendous support from the Periscope community as a whole. My "periscope success" inspired me to dream more and reach for more because there is always a next level that can be accomplished.

As always, special thanks to my editor, Brooke-Sidney J. Harbour. I love you like a sister. Your ability to transform my work amazes me. God bless.

To everyone who I met on my online journey, thank you for playing a role in my life. And to all of you who are a part of my offline life, I appreciate you. And I appreciate the fact that our parts crossed. I love you all.

Triumph!

ABOUT THE AUTHOR

Nkechi Ajaeroh, MPH is a two-time, International Bestselling Author, top-rated "healthy" productivity success mentor and advocate, speaker, Periscope broadcaster, and an extraordinary home cook. She is fondly referred to as the queen of "getting things done." She is also a former reservist in the United Stated Army, a mother and a military wife. She went from living an unfulfilling life to an extraordinary life, becoming an Amazon number one bestselling author with her first and second book, "Elevate Your Life with the Power of Positive Perception: What I Now Know for Sure," and Gratefully Growing: Gaining Ground with Gratitude. Nkechi gets things done with her daily intentional living strategies.

To say this woman is multi-talented and versatile is an understatement. She currently hosts a very successful cooking show on Periscope, "Bringing Nigerian Food Near You," where she teaches viewers how to make favorite Nigerian dishes.

She is passionate about girls' education, which is still on the back burner in many countries around the world. As a little girl growing up in the Imo state of Nigeria, Nkechi loved school. Her love of education is why she continues to support the girls' education initiative.

Nkechi Ajaeroh's company, Just Positude Co. LLC, is a positive attitude company determined to change the world – one good deed at a time. The Just Positude blog (www.justpositude.com) is an educational and inspirational website that helps multitasking, multi-passionate, high-achievers streamline and strategize their goals for optimal success by mastering the art of productivity. The site helps her readers accomplish their goals, have more free time, be happy, and most importantly, achieve everything without losing their minds. Her personal blog (www.nkechiajaeroh.com) is a food and lifestyle blog that inspires you to use your wings while sharing her Nigerian recipes and inspiration.

Nkechi's lifetime and global goal is to inspire, motivate, educate and empower men and women to know their worth so they can use their wings. She helps people see and embrace growth through consistent, intentional action. She is now on a mission to help you to create and achieve life-changing goals because when you start, you must finish successfully.

ALSO AVAILABLE FROM NKECHI AJAEROH:

Elevate Your Life with the Power of Positive Perception: What I Now Know for Sure.
Nkechi Ajaeroh's FIRST BOOK is a powerful positivity tool. Learn how to live a more fulfilling life by refocusing on the things that matter.

Get it here: https://nkechiajaeroh.com/shop/

Gratefully Growing: Gaining Ground with Gratitude

is Nkechi Ajaeroh's second book. It encourages you to look at every struggle as a growing experience.

Get it here: https://nkechiajaeroh.com/shop/

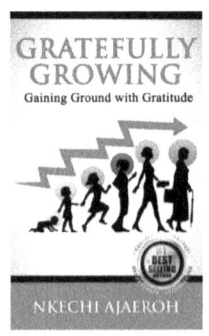

www.ingramcontent.com/pod-product-compliance
Lightning Source LLC
Chambersburg PA
CBHW070551100426
42744CB00006B/258